Kilkenny College, the school of Swift, Congreve, Prior and Berkeley, founded in 1538.

the *Essay* as a pioneering work on perception.

It is in the *Principles*, however, that Berkeley makes his telling philosophical arguments. It is the 'mother lode' of his thought. It becomes the complete and final expression of his major principle, *esse is percipi* – to be is to be perceived. There are but two factors: 1. mind; 2. perception.

An object existing in itself, neither perceiving nor perceived, is meaningless. It is not that the 'perceived object' goes away. It is simply that there is no need for a level of existence between the 'object of the senses' and the perceivers of it. The tree does not cease to exist on the quad when not perceived by 'you or I' since, according to Berkeley, the mind of God *is* about in the quad, as Ronald Knox's famous limerick told us,

> *There once was a man who said 'God*
> *Must think it exceedingly odd*
>   *If he finds that this tree*
>   *Continues to be*
> *When there's no one about in the*
>   *Quad.'*

and the reply,

> *Dear Sir,*
>   *your astonishment's odd:*
> *I am always about in the Quad.*
>   *And that's why the tree*
>   *Will continue to be*
> *Since observed by,*
>   *Yours faithfully,*
>   *God.*

Needless to say, the reaction to Berkeley's idea was quick and negative; confused would be the better description.

The *Dialogues* was an attempt by Berkeley to clarify and perhaps simplify the *Principles*. In the dialogue style of Plato he proceeds to cover all of the points developed in the *Principles*, but in a style more understandable to the lay reader.

Passive Obedience, also written during this period, is a work on ethics and political theory motivated by the political uncertainties of the time and dealing with questions of authority and compliance. Queen Anne had no heir, and the Old Pretender, Anne's half-brother, was in the background. The question of her successor was foremost in the minds of the citizenry and the issue had led to the most severe of the penal code excesses in Ireland. With Anne having no child of her own, the Protestant ascendancy in Ireland was highly anxious over the question of succession and seeking to assure their continued control. It could hardly be said that Berkeley's writings were restricted to abstract themes. It was the equivalent of the most learned of contemporary philosophers commenting on the present political state of Northern Ireland.

In addition to his enormous literary output Berkeley continued his duties at Trinity. He served as Librarian of the College during the period when plans

Front Square of Trinity College with the Campanile in the centre and the Rubrics, oldest building in College in the background.

The World of George Berkeley

Raymond W. Houghton

There is a certain irony in George Berkeley's birth on 12 March 1685 near Kilkenny, and his childhood at Dysart Castle near Thomastown on the River Nore.

The building, a modest stone structure set in the midst of a broad field sloping from the Thomastown to Inistioge road is surrounded by great trees, surely some of which have survived the three centuries since. The Nore gushes past, splitting the vale. An ancient salmon weir, still operative, monitors the flow before the site. The ruins of the house seem fixed on one end to an older structure. The ivy-covered keep of the castle itself, standing awaiting the available funds to prevent its imminent collapse, is there yet. Far across the valley in view from the house and castle stands Brandon Hill, named after St Brendan the Navigator whose epic voyage took him westward across the Atlantic where Berkeley was to go, where, in the words of Berkeley's celebrated poem *Westward the course of Empire (was to take) its Way*.

The family, well-to-do by the standards of the time, had probably been in Ireland since the Restoration. Certainly George Berkeley thought of himself as Irish for he was to describe himself thus many times: '*We Irishmen*' he was to write.

At ten years of age Berkeley entered Kilkenny College, proudly called by some 'the Eton of Ireland', founded in 1538 by the Earl of Ormonde. Swift studied there before him, as did William Congreve. He was a classmate of Thomas Prior, his lifelong friend and correspondent and a founder of the Royal Dublin Society. Kilkenny, perhaps the Irish city least changed since Berkeley's time, is the site of the notable cathedral of St Canice with its adjacent round tower and the great castle of the Ormondes beside the Nore which overlooks the school itself.

We know little of his time at Kilkenny save his exploration with schoolmates of the Cave of Dunmore, four miles from Kilkenny, with its tunnels reaching deep beneath the surface of the countryside. The cave remains a public attraction recognisable from Berkeley's description of it contained in a surviving essay he was to write later, while at Trinity College.

In 1700, at the age of fifteen, he matriculated at Trinity College, Dublin. The city, founded as a Viking settlement, had long since extended beyond its original walls so that the College, having already celebrated its centenary, was well integrated into its rapidly expanding life. Fifty thousand people populated Dublin. The decade had been tumultuous. It had seen the challenge of James II and his defeat at the Boyne by William of Orange though the ascent of Queen Anne to the throne was yet to come. Berkeley's time at Trinity would continue for the next twenty-four years: he studied classics, Hebrew, logic and theology. We know of his exposure to Locke and to Malebranche which helped to trigger his startling doctrine of immaterialism. He took the Bachelor of Arts degree in 1704, not yet twenty years of age, and, like many promising scholars of his day, properly considered the awarding of the degree the commencement of study and remained to continue his work.

Already his probings, which would lead to his major philosophical contributions, had begun. The following three years, leading to his election as Junior Fellow of the College in 1707, were the germinal years of his intellectual development. His philosophical musings which were to emerge more fully shaped in his major writings may be traced in his notebooks (more accurately intellectual diaries) that he kept during these years. Fraser, the great nineteenth-century Berkeley scholar, discovered and published them as *The Commonplace Book, occasional Metaphysical Thoughts*, but it remained for the greatest of all Berkeley scholars, A. A. Luce of Trinity College, to order them and to rename the collection the *Philosophical Commentaries*. In rapid order the publications appeared: *An essay towards a New Theory of Vision*, 1709; *A treatise concerning the principles of human knowledge, Part I*, 1710; and *Three Dialogues between Hyas and Philonous*, 1713. The contribution of one of these works would have given an author stature, but the three in four years was a prodigious output.

A New Theory of Vision, considered a classic by psychologists as well as philosophers, stakes out part of his immaterialist position. For the western world it was the era of new development in eyeglasses, telescopes and microscopes, the technology of vision. A new theory of vision was called for. Berkeley distinguishes between what we actually see, modes of light and colour, and what we think we see or infer. The *Essay* takes the visible world into the mind and leaves the tangible world outside. Modern psychologists continue to read

Kilkenny Castle, the historic seat of the Ormondes, overlooking the River Nore.

Bishop Berkeley *by John Vanderbank. This portrait (1734) painted shortly after the publication of Alciphron and his appointment as Bishop of Cloyne is in the possession of Trinity College, Dublin.*

were under way for the new Library designed by Thomas Burgh and built between the years 1713 and 1732. This is now referred to as the Old Library, which is considered to be one of the greatest tourist attractions in Ireland. The Book of Kells is displayed in the Long Room of the Library. Berkeley was also Junior Dean of the College, in charge of College discipline, during what were uneasy days in Dublin and in College.

Having accomplished his monumental philosophical task, Berkeley began to explore his world. He obtained a queen's letter permitting him two years of time away from Dublin. Bearing the manuscript of the *Dialogues* he left Ireland for the first time, at the age of twenty-eight. By ferry he sailed for Holyhead and travelled the conventional route through Chester and Coventry to London. He was not overly impressed. In a letter to Lord Percival he finds that 'London itself seems to exceed Dublin not so much in the stateliness or beauty of the buildings as in extent.'

Percival and the aforementioned

The Lecture *(1736) by Hogarth. Students attending a lecture on the subject of a vacuum.* **Facing page:** *The Long room of the Old Library, Trinity College, built between the years 1713 and 1732.*

Thomas Prior were to become Berkeley's principal correspondents and it is primarily through their letters that we are able to follow Berkeley's movements and plans. Sir John Percival, the first Lord of Egmont, was heir to the title and estates of his father who had served under Cromwell in Ireland. Berkeley dedicated the *Essay on Vision* to Percival, who was known as a landlord of conscience, sympathetic to Ireland. He was to describe Berkeley as 'a man of noblest virtues, best learning I ever knew.'

Berkeley was an immediate hit in London; his ten months there were filled by enriching experiences as he entered into the life of the London wits. His reputation had preceded him and he was sought out by Richard Steele, the essayist and publisher. Percival's friends and relatives greeted him and he became a friend of the Earl of Pembroke, former Lord Lieutenant of Ireland, who would later support his Bermuda scheme. From letters to Percival we learn of Berkeley's adventures. His name appeared in Jonathan Swift's

Journal and in Pope's letters and verse.

He attended the theatre with Addison; he dined with Lord Berkeley of Stratton; he published the *Dialogues*; he spent a week with Pope at Twickenham and advised him on *Essay on Man*. Pope was to immortalise Berkeley in the verse: 'To Berkeley ev'ry virtue under heav'n'; he charmed Arbuthnot, the queen's physician; and he became friends with the poets Gay and Parnell. Steele, who was Dublin born, knew Berkeley's writings and was hospitable to him, 'even though he has heard I am a Tory.' Berkeley contributed more than a dozen articles to Steele's *Guardian*. Published anonymously, they were largely attacks on 'freethinking'.

Swift, eighteen years older than Berkeley, introduced him at Court and obtained residence for him. Their names were to be associated for the rest of Swift's life. Undoubtedly they had met in Dublin and Swift probably had read the *Essay on Vision*; Luce attributes the notion of relativity in size in *Gulliver's Travels* to Swift's reading of the *Essay on Vision*. Swift was to praise and support Berkeley throughout his life and Berkeley was certainly to reciprocate, but although they are known to

Title page and illustration from 1727 edition of Swift's Gulliver's Travels.

have corresponded, no letters survive.

Berkeley left London in the autumn of 1713. He travelled as chaplain with Lord Peterborough – Swift had arranged it – on his first European journey of ten months. He landed at Calais after a dangerous voyage, the result of 'the hazards that attend rash and ignorant seamen.' He travelled across France to Paris, visiting the Louvre, the Sorbonne and various convents and monasteries. Luce believes that he visited the famed philosopher monk, Malebranche, shortly before Malebranche's death. Certainly influenced by him, Berkeley debated heatedly with Malebranche on 'certain points' but Luce assures us that Berkeley's visit was not the cause of the priest's death.

In Paris he witnessed the erection of a statue to the king with speeches and fireworks. Leaving Paris for Italy, riding post over rocks and mountains almost impassable with ice and snow, and coming off with 'only four falls from which I received no other damage then the breaking of my sword, my watch and my snuffbox,' he crossed Mount Cenis, the most dangerous part of the Alps, on New Year's Eve.

He was three weeks in Genoa, which Berkeley found magnificent. In Leghorn, Joseph Stock his first biographer tells that, on the day following his preaching a sermon, priests entered a room paying no heed of him as they marched around the room praying. Berkeley thought it a visit from the Inquisition to punish his unauthorised preaching. He was relieved to find that it was the day for blessing the house against rats and mice. Returning to Paris, he travelled through Flanders and Holland to England which he reached at about the time of Queen Anne's death.

After two years in England and a brief visit to Ireland, Berkeley returned to Italy again, this time as tutor to George Ashe. Once more crossing the Alps in winter, Berkeley describes his encounter with a wolf.

A huge dark-coloured wolf ran across an open plain, when our chaise was passing, when he came near as he turned about and made a stand with a very fierce and daring look. I instantly drew my sword and Mr Ashe fired his pistol. I did the same, upon which the beast very calmly retired looking

Bishop Berkeley *by James Latham.*
This portrait appears on the Irish
airmail stamp issued in 1985 to
commemorate the Berkeley
Tercentenary.

Dublin Bay in the early eighteenth century.

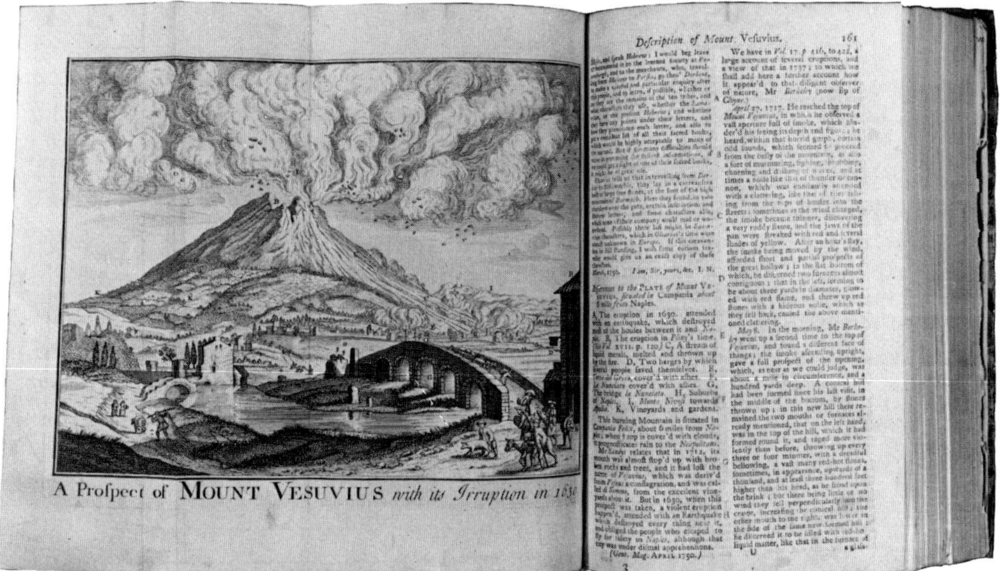

Illustration of Mount Vesuvius with Berkeley's description of an eruption in the right-hand column.

back ever and anon. We were much mortified that he did not attack us, and give us an opportunity of killing him.

His letters describe his travels in Italy in great detail. Berkeley commented on the art, viewed the Pantheon and criticised the absence of galleries in some cities. He described the procession of the Pope. He climbed Vesuvius and watched an eruption which he detailed for Sir John Arbuthnot, who communicated the account to the Royal Society. He kept a log in great detail while riding in the chaise. His diary commented on tarantism, then a matter of interest throughout Europe, particularly among physicians. It was said that the bite of the tarantula caused pathological disorders which were relieved by music and dance. In letters to Pope and Percival he described the sights of Naples and the beauties of the island of Ischia. From Sicily he wrote of earthquakes and described the classical remains on the island which seemed to have influenced him greatly. On his return journey he wrote a Latin tract *De Motu* which he submitted to the Royal Academy in Paris. It continues to be read by physicists and, to some, anticipates Albert Einstein. He returned to London late in 1720.

Berkeley had taken orders in the Church of Ireland in 1709. On returning to Trinity College in 1721, he took the degrees of B.D. and D.D. and was appointed Divinity lecturer. During his absence he had succeeded to Senior Fellow and was thus deeply involved in the government of the College. He was also called upon to advise on the design and construction of Castletown, the residence-to-be of Speaker Connolly, 'the finest (house) Ireland ever saw.'

In 1722 the position of Dean of Derry became vacant and after fierce political and ecclesiastical infighting, Berkeley was appointed to the position. He was installed in May 1724, in turn resigning his Senior Fellowship and ending twenty-four years of association with Trinity College. He never took up residence in Derry. Although he provided for the affairs of the church there, his main interest was in matters far from that place.

Undoubtedly the plans had been simmering within him for some time: his European tours had prepared him. The evidence is clear. His *Essay towards preventing the ruine of Great Britain* warned of the need for 'religion, industry, frugality and public spirit' to counteract the 'calamities of the South Sea Project.' He attacked luxury of dress and degenerate life and called for economic reforms and attention to the spiritual value of the arts. He saw Europe in a state of moral decay.

A scheme emerged in his mind and developed into a passion. It is certain that by 1721 he had made a decision. It was announced to Lord Percival in May of 1722. He told Percival that the plans had been in his mind for ten months and that he was determined 'to spend the residue of my days in the Island of Bermuda' where it was his intention to establish a college to educate the 'youth of our plantations' in order to supply churches with pastors. He would also educate 'young American Savages' through the Master of Arts degree to become missionaries to their own people.

Why Bermuda? In a continent without roads, he saw the island on a sea route as halfway between the northern and southern colonies. He felt that Bermuda would be healthy, comfortable, secure and would not 'tempt men from their studies to turn traders.'

Berkeley informed Percival that he had already recruited a dozen gentlemen to accompany him and raised the prospect of a truly utopian community where one might 'live with pleasure and dignity for £5 per annum.' He invited Percival and his lady to accompany him. He anticipated the era of romantic Utopianism which developed over the next century in Britain and throughout Europe.

The reaction to the scheme was immediate. Some considered it insane. Others were enthusiastic. Berkeley sold the plan with unwavering zeal. The

The Sir Christopher Wren Building, College of William and Mary in Virginia.

reputation of Bermuda as an earthly paradise was already well known in European circles. Unfortunately for Berkeley his geography was inexact, for Bermuda's location was to prove one of the major downfalls in his scheme.

Yet initially he had powerful support. Swift endorsed the plan; the Bishop of London, Dr Arbuthnot, the Dean of Chichester, the Duke of Newcastle, London bankers, the Archbishop of Canterbury all were supporters. Berkeley obtained the king's approval and

Berkeley was consulted on the design of Castletown House, Co. Kildare, built by Speaker Conolly.

that of the Parliament. He even obtained the funding through financial subscribers who pledged £3,400. He discovered that land on the island of St Christopher in the West Indies was to be sold following the ceding of the island under the Treaty of Utrecht. He sought to obtain £20,000 of these funds for the College. A friend from his Italian trip, Abbe Gaulteri, took Berkeley's proposal to King George I who directed Sir Robert Walpole to bring it to the House of Commons where there were

but two open dissenters. Berkeley received his charter and the promise of £20,000 to pursue the plan for a college in Bermuda.

In addition, one of the strangest coincidences in the saga had provided an additional £2,000. He had been left that sum in the will of Hester van Homrigh, Swift's Vanessa. Hester, apparently provoked because Swift had rejected her, struck Swift from her will and made Berkeley, who had scarcely known her, a beneficiary of her estate.

Present day view of Newport, Rhode Island. Harbour with transatlantic racing trimaran and eighteenth-century reproduction sailing vessel behind. **Facing page:** *Trinity Church in Newport, Rhode Island, where Berkeley often preached while in America.*

Berkeley saw this as a sign of divine approval and, although the parliamentary grant was not immediately forthcoming, prepared for his departure to America.

Just before leaving Berkeley married Anne Forster, daughter of John Forster, Speaker of the Irish House of Commons and Lord Chief Justice.

I chose her for the qualities of her mind and her unaffected inclination to books. She goes with great cheerfulness to live a plain farmer's life and wears stuff of her own spinning wheel.

Reverend James Honyman, rector of Trinity Church, Newport, host and friend of Berkeley.

Berkeley chartered a vessel and with his wife, John James, Richard Dalton, John Smibert (who was to become America's first portrait painter) and Miss Handcock they sailed from Gravesend in September 1728. Aboard were books and supplies to begin St Paul's College. There was no announcement of the departure and no public leave-taking.

The ship was 'a long time blundering about the ocean', but eventually reached Virginia where they were received as honoured guests. Although Percival's friend William Byrd was absent, we know of Berkeley's time there through Byrd's long letter to Percival. He visited the College of William and Mary and dined with the governor, but after a short stay they continued on to Rhode Island and arrived in Newport on 23 January 1729.

Yesterday arrived here Dean Berkeley of Londonderry in a pretty large ship. He is a gentleman of middle stature, of an agreeable, pleasant, and erect aspect. He was ushered into the town with a great number of gentlemen, to whom he behaved himself after a very complaisant manner. 'Tis said he purposes to tarry here with his family about three months.

Berkeley sent this organ as a gift to Trinity Church after his return.

News of the imminent arrival was brought to the Reverend Honyman of Trinity Church while he was in the pulpit, at which point the church was dismissed with a blessing and Mr Honyman with wardens, vestry and congregation, male and female, repaired immediately to the Ferry Wharf where the party arrived a little before the Dean, his family and friends.

Newport was at the time one of the principal cities of the Colonies. It had a population of five to six thousand people. It was a leading mercantile centre and a leading seaport in the Colonies. Berkeley himself described it. He reported the landscape to provide 'delightful prospects'. He found the population to include 'Anabaptists . . . Presbyterians, Quakers, Independents and . . . no persuasion at all.' There were 'fewer quarrels about religion than elsewhere' and 'people (lived) peaceably with their neighbours, of whatever profession.' He found Newport 'the most thriving place in all America for its bigness. . . . I was never more agreeably surprised than at the first sight of the town and its harbour.'

Berkeley was welcomed with enthu-siasm. His reputation had preceded him. The Berkeleys spent the first weeks living with the Honymans. Trinity Church was considered the finest church between New York and Boston. It is still standing and has remained one of the most influential Episcopal churches in America. Berkeley preached the first of his many sermons in Trinity three days after his arrival. His sermons were popular with the inhabitants, and members of all the sects of Newport came to hear him. In one sermon he proclaimed: 'Give the devil his due, John Calvin was a great man.' Newport was prosperous. The men tended to wear 'flaming scarlet coats and waistcoats, laced and fringed with the brightest glaring yellow.'

Soon after his arrival Berkeley sought to obtain a house near Newport as a residence for his family while awaiting news of his grant and for later use as a base of supplies for the College in Bermuda. He negotiated the purchase of a farm of about ninety-six acres in the adjacent town of Middletown. There were buildings on the place but apparently he designed and had constructed the comfortable farmhouse

Woodcut of 'Savages' in America. Actually, the colonials had all but destroyed native American culture in Rhode Island fifty years before Berkeley's arrival.
Below: *Whitehall, Berkeley's house in Middletown, Rhode Island, built by him and left to Yale University on his departure. It is now maintained by the Society of Colonial Dames in America.*

which survives to this day. He named it Whitehall and by the end of April he moved in and remained for a period of over two years.

His time was well spent. Although he avoided a public life, he continued to preach at Trinity. He journeyed across the Bay to the Narragansett Country on the mainland, where he visited the missionary priest, Reverend James McSparren, his wife Hannah and the Updyke family. He preached at McSparren's church where McSparren, also an Irishman, is said to have been able to preach in the Irish language. McSparren brought him to visit the native Americans who were still living there, survivors of the Indian Wars of 1674. Berkeley and McSparren got on well, and he was to make many trips to what then seemed the wilds of the colonial interior.

Reverend James McSparran, Irish born and Irish speaking, rector of St Paul's Church in Rhode Island, friend of Berkeley in America.

St Paul's Church, Wichford, Rhode Island. This was Reverend James McSparran's mission church on the 'mainland' side of Narragansett Bay. Berkeley preached in this building.

He was influential in the intellectual life of Rhode Island and was a force behind the founding of the Philosophical Society which organised the Redwood Library, one of the oldest libraries in America. He entertained clergy from Connecticut and Massachusetts as well as Rhode Island, the most famous of whom, the Reverend Samuel Johnson of Connecticut, was to become the first president of what is now Columbia University. Johnson had already known of Berkeley's work and was to emerge as one of the New World's most distinguished early philosophers.

All the while waiting for news of the availability of his £20,000 from Parliament, Berkeley continued his writing and completed *Alciphron or the Minute Philosopher*, another work in dialogue form, in defence of Christianity against the encroachment of free thinking. Descriptions of Rhode Island appear in the work and it is said that the characters represent people he knew in Newport.

His mail arrived at the White Horse Tavern, now the oldest continuously operating tavern in America. His correspondence betrays his diminishing hope of ever receiving his grant and his realisation that the Bermuda venture was a mistake. He considered building the College in Rhode Island but was afraid that if such a thought were to surface in England the entire plan might be more easily scuttled.

I have wrote to some friends in England to take proper steps for procuring a translation of the College from Bermuda to Rhode Island as soon as the 20,000 pounds arising by sale of lands in St Christopher's is paid to our order, and I have furnished them with the weightiest reasons that occurred for so doing, but I don't think it advisable to make this proposition, or say anything about it before the money is received.
I am here in no small anxiety waiting the event of things.

A son was born to the Berkeleys during these weeks. Undoubtedly the birth and the christening of the infant, Henry, in September did much to brighten the lives of the Berkeleys.

Samuel Johnston of Connecticut, Berkeley's leading philosophical disciple. They visited often in America. He later became the first president of Columbia University.

Engraving of a portrait of Berkeley, after his consecration as Bishop in Lambeth Palace. Artist unknown, but very probably painted by an Irish artist in the middle 1730s.

But the discouragement continued. Berkeley waited hopefully for better news from England.

I live here upon land I have purchased, and in a farmhouse that I have built on this Island. It is fit for cows and sheep and may be of good use for supplying our College at

St Colman's Cathedral and Round Tower in Cloyne, Co. Cork, site of Berkeley's bishopric.

Bermuda. Mr James, Dalton and Smibert, etc. are at Boston, and have been there for several months. My wife and I abide by Rhode Island, preferring quiet and solitude to the noise of a great town, notwithstanding all the solicitations that have been used to draw us thither.

I am now employing the interest of my friends in England; and have wrote in the most pressing manner either to get the money paid, or at least to get a positive answer that may direct me what course I am to take.

But the money was never to come as the scheme, although supported by the king and Parliament, had powerful opponents. Lord Townsend opposed the plan on the basis that dependencies should be kept dependent and another lord is alleged to have said that not only should there be no college in the New World, there probably should have never been one in Dublin.

The Bishop of London approached Walpole about the question. Walpole's answer was the dropping of the axe:

If you put this question to me as a Minister, I must and can assure you that the money shall most undoubtedly be paid as soon as suits with public convenience; but if you ask me as a friend whether Dean Berkeley should continue in America, expecting the payment of £20,000, I advise him by all means to return home to Europe, and to give up his present expectations.

The word came to Berkeley and he accepted it. Plans were drawn to leave Rhode Island. He decided to leave his books and his estate to the then young and struggling College at New Haven (Yale). He baptised and freed his three slaves. He disposed of most of his personal property as his party would be sailing back to England as passengers, not aboard a chartered vessel.

A second child, Lucia, but a few weeks old, died on 6 September 1732 and was buried in the Trinity Church graveyard.

They left Newport for the forty-mile overland trip to Boston where Berkeley had opportunity to visit Harvard College, founded in 1636. He would later provide Harvard with a library of the classics.

On 21 September they sailed from Boston aboard Captain Carlin's ship and after an uneventful voyage arrived on 20 October 1732.

Certainly there was no shame in the failure of the Bermuda plan and Berkeley felt none. Had the money been forthcoming, had he decided to build the College in Rhode Island, the course of history might have been changed. As it was, Berkeley brought a spark to the New World. He was undoubtedly the most distinguished visitor from Europe to set foot in the New World. He provided an intellectual uplift to life in the colonies. While he founded no college of his own, he influenced Yale, Harvard, Columbia, Pennsylvania, the College of William and Mary and, indirectly, the future course of higher education in America. Indeed, he is thought of as the 'Father of Higher Education' in America. There are Berkeley placenames in California, Massachusetts, Rhode Island, and numerous other places in the United States. He had devoted eleven years of his life to the planning and execution of his dream.

During the period following his return he wrote *The Analyst, or a discourse addressed to an infidel mathematician*, which is partly a refutation of Newton's doctrine of fluxions although Newton is not personally identified as the 'infidel'. The work generated considerable controversy among mathematicians, although it was in part a defence of the 'mysteries' of Christianity.

Within two years of his return, with the help and support of the Lord Lieutenant of Ireland and the queen herself, Berkeley was made Bishop of Cloyne. Cloyne, in the County of Cork, was an ancient ecclesiastical centre said to have been founded by St Colman in the sixth century. The cathedral is named after him. Cloyne today seems little changed from the village in which Berkeley spent the last nineteen years of his life. From the top of the round tower in the centre of town one still looks out over gently rolling farmland in all directions.

Berkeley's years of service in Cloyne were not interrupted other than a short period in Dublin to assume his position in the Irish House of Lords and a visit to Killarney. He remained within his diocese until his departure for Oxford shortly before his death. The years were pastoral, certainly. There was devotion to his flock and to the community at large. He continued to write and to maintain his correspondence with Prior and Percival. He also wrote to Isaac Gervais with whom he exchanged a series of cheerful personal letters which show us a rather different, lighter side of Berkeley. He maintained his ties with America continuing contact with Samuel Johnson and the presidents of Harvard and Yale.

He was interested in the affairs of his time. While in Dublin he wrote *A discourse addressed to Magistrates and Men in Authority* in which he attacked

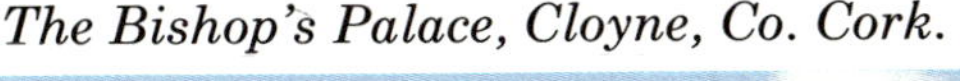

The Bishop's Palace, Cloyne, Co. Cork.

Christ Church, Oxford where Berkeley is buried. Berkeley died while in Oxford overseeing the education of his son, George.

the Blasters, a society whom he accuses of 'a train of studied, deliberate indignities against the divine Majesty'. Tradition associates the Blasters with the so-called Hell Fire Club which had a headquarters in the Dublin mountains, the remains of which may still be seen. During the rising of 1745, when Bonnie Prince Charlie marched on London and caused consternation throughout the islands, Berkley raised a force of military in the event of the extension of the rebellion to Ireland. He entertained in the palace at Cloyne and sponsored musical evenings. He personally supervised the education of his three sons and his daughter.

Apparently his relationship with his wife Anne was idyllic. She was an artist, a fine singer, made her own clothes, supervised the farm, had mystic interests and was herself an accomplished writer. A letter to her son about her husband is a loyal and tender tribute to him.

Dean Swift in all likelihood visited Berkeley at Cloyne as did many other notables of the day. Strangest of all his visitors perhaps was the 'Irish Giant', Cornelius McGrath, a lad of fifteen years and seven feet nine and three quarter inches tall, who spent a month with Berkeley.

The Bishop established a spinning school at Cloyne. He set up a system of public works; he gave money to the poor.

To feed the hungry and clothe the naked by promoting an honest indus-

Recumbent figure of Berkeley in memorial room in St Colman's Cathedral, Cloyne, Co. Cork.

try is not unproper employment for a clergyman who still thinks himself as a member of the commonwealth.

With Swift, Berkeley was a patriotic, if colonial, nationalist. During his time at Cloyne Berkeley wrote *The Querist*, a series of 595 questions in the last edition, which cleverly raised consciousness about issues of the time. It slightly criticised and commented on governmental policy, the Church, wealth, industry, drinking, public works, trade, and even Trinity College. It shows Berkeley's keen knowledge of basic economics and public policy. It remains a prophetic and seminal piece of writing and it is worth noting that both De Valera and Jack Lynch, former prime ministers of Ireland, have quoted Berkeley and cited him an early visionary with respect to economics and politics.

Life was difficult at Cloyne. There was sickness and disease and infirmity with no doctors, nor hospitals, nor medical supplies, nor proper hygiene. Around 1740 Berkeley, deeply disturbed at the misery about him, began his experiments with tar water. Whether he first heard about it on his European travels or in America (from the native Americans or from the South Carolineans in Newport) is impossible to say, but experiment he did. He took it himself as a preventative for dysentery. He gave it to his own family and neighbours and mentioned it in a note to the *Dublin Journal*.

In 1744 he published *Siris*, probably

Professor A. A. Luce, of Trinity College, Dublin, greatest Berkeley scholar of the twentieth century.

the best selling of all his books, in which he described the virtues of tar water and provided descriptions of its manufacture and use. Tar water became an instant success. Edmund Burke from Dublin commented: 'I am sure tar is the most universal medicine here, notwithstanding the opposition of its enemies.' Cures were reported for a variety of complaints. Berkeley himself thought it might well be the universal cure. One is reminded of the contemporary claims of success for vitamin C as a universal cure. *Siris* was not merely a treatise on tar water, however. It is a rather strange, almost mystical work, that deals with the 'vital spirit of the world.'

In July of 1752, in poor health, Berkeley moved with his wife and daughter to Oxford to supervise his son George's university education. He had a house on Holywell Street near the gardens of New College. It was in that house that Berkeley died in January 1753. He was with his family, his wife reading from the Bible, his daughter pouring his tea, his son George beside him. He died peacefully, and was buried, as his will had directed, in the parish of his demise. He was interred in Christ Church Cathedral, which is the chapel of the college of the same name, on 20 January. Professor Luce says,

During his lifetime (Berkeley) was honoured in his own country and in his own university and he is honoured there still; but he belonged, and belongs, also to a wider world.